A Special Place

Featuring the Images of Mary Donovan

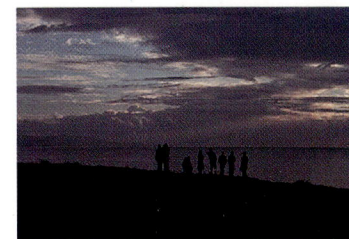

A SPECIAL PLACE

Library of Congress Catalogue No. 97-094158

ISBN: 0-9647561-3-7

1. Palos Verdes Peninsula 2. Photography
3. Seascapes and Landscapes

This Limited Edition published by LIBRIS BOOKS CO.
Torrance, CA

Printed and published in the United States.

A Special Place

A Picture Story of the Palos Verdes Peninsula

By Mary Donovan and Ted Bruinsma

Authors' Comments

Our objective in composing the picture book of the Palos Verdes Peninsula was to share with the reader, through photography, the scenic beauty, natural environment, and unique lifestyle that make the Peninsula "A Special Place." In doing so we have attempted to combine the professional photographic experience of Mary with the project planning and publication experience of Ted.

Our efforts will be rewarded if all past, present and potential residents and their friends—through the book—enjoy the allure of the Palos Verdes Peninsula.

Mary Donovan

Ted Bruinsma

Cover Photo:
The Point Vicente Lighthouse, located near Long Point, is one of the most important lighthouses on the West Coast. See inside for picture and complete text.

Foreword

There are many nice places where people can live in America, and more than a few of them are in California. However, it requires something more than being "nice" to be special. One such special place is the Palos Verdes Peninsula.

Fewer than 15 miles from the Los Angeles airport, down the coast from the wide sandy shores of Manhattan, Hermosa and Redondo Beaches, the Peninsula gallantly juts out into the Pacific Ocean, proud of its scenic wonders, its awesome seascapes and its rolling hills.

Throughout the years, the Peninsula has had a rich history of Spanish Land Grants, extensive cattle operations, and early land barons who sought to exploit the resources of the rare, then open, acres. One dream has remained constant for all these years, even in the face of inevitable development. Today that constant dream—that this land must become and remain the perfect community—is The Special Place that is named the Palos Verdes Peninsula.

Although just twenty-five miles from the megalopolis of Los Angeles, whose downtown buildings can be seen on the horizon, the Peninsula has reserved, to a remarkable degree, the care-free enjoyment of the simple things that make life a paradise. From the port town of San Pedro with its harbor and famous lighthouse, past sprawling country estates and a panorama of dwellings and craggy bluffs with wind-swept hills, throughout charming rural communities, tree-lined streets and red-tiled roofs, the Peninsula has enveloped itself in an atmosphere of relaxed well-being that one can feel—and almost touch. Here is a place of natural charm where people have deliberately cultivated isolation and tranquility.

An Introduction

In 1913, New York investors purchased much of the Peninsula, intending to create a community of large estates for the wealthy. Several years later, the Palos Verdes Estate Project was founded by Frank A. Vanderlip, Sr., one of the early investors, and E.G. Lewis, a real estate developer.

Soon the first houses appeared and "The Rancho" become known as the Palos Verdes Peninsula. Today, almost fully developed, the Peninsula has been divided into four independent cities: Rolling Hills, Palos Verdes Estates, Rolling Hills Estates, and Rancho Palos Verdes.

In our picture book, we have added San Pedro and the Los Angeles harbor, whose particular beauty is part of the original Peninsula.

Rancho Palos Verdes

The entire Palos Verdes Peninsula can be described as a collection of vista points of many spectacular views. Overshadowing them all are the beautiful scenes from Rancho Palos Verdes to the south. The nine-mile drive along the shoreline offers sweeping views of the ocean waves crashing against the craggy coastline, in and out of often inaccessible coves. Frequent long, wing-like reaches of land project into the sea creating tiny bays that sometimes seem separated only by salty, foamy sprays. One is treated to a magnificent spectacle where all the horizon is the ocean, stretching as far as imagination and thought can go. History and romance have named the sites most easily reached.

From Hawthorne Boulevard, looking south, the Rancho Palos Verdes Coastline. St. Peter's Church can be seen on the right.

Inspiration Point with Smuggler's Cove in the foreground.

The sea.

The tide pools at Abalone Cove.

Peninsula fog at sunrise.

Portuguese Point with Long Point, site of the former Marineland, in the background.

As land values grew on the Peninsula and cattle ranching was no longer feasible, land was leased to Japanese farmers for cultivation of flowers, vegetables, and grains. From the early 1950's until 1992, Annie Ishibashi offered fresh produce and flowers to Peninsula residents. Regular trips to "Annie's Stand," now operated by her husband, Jimmy, and her daughter, Yvonne, are still on many shopping calendars.

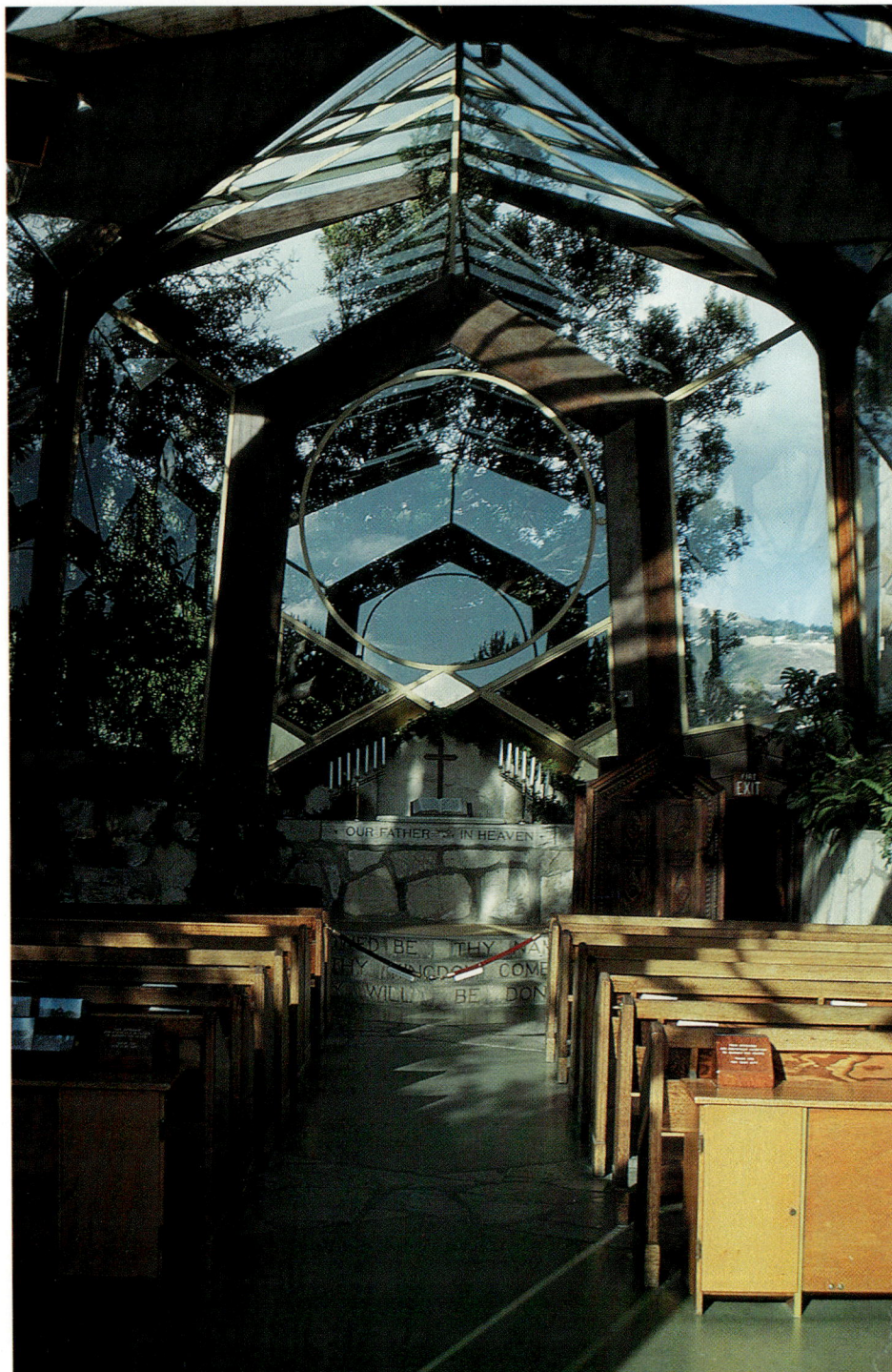

The Glass Church

Nestled in the floral splendor of the Palos Verdes hills, overlooking the Pacific, is the nationally renowned Wayfarer's Chapel. Here the genius of Frank Lloyd Wright unites the natural and the spiritual through the commingling of glass, stone and redwood grandeur. Dedicated in 1951 as a monument to Emanuel Swedenborg, the three and one-half acres contain a 59 ft. bell tower, a library, museum, and a cloister. An abundance of flowering plants and trees with biblical significance embrace a natural amphitheater.

The historic Portuguese Bend Cove—named after two Portuguese whaling companies that operated there for many years. The area is now more famous for its reactivated and devastating land movement that has continued, unabated, since 1956.

Oh Catalina!

The Island of Catalina, an hour away by boat, at dusk
seems to float magically on the horizon.

The Casino Ballroom at Catalina, where big bands and
musical festivals have entertained since 1920.

The Point Vicente Lighthouse

To the land traveler, the many views of the Pacific Ocean are electrifying. The waters can be strikingly blue as they capture the sky. The sea will alternate between being smooth and glassy or the spawner of treacherous waves that beat angrily upon rugged shores. The view from land starts with a glorious rising of the sun and ends at dusk as the sun sets its own majestic display of reflections and colors.

The seaman from his deck shares not this beauty but rather deplores the dangerous channels that in years gone by have claimed many vessels as their victims. How shallow the seascapes can be!

For Master and Crew alike, the Point Vicente Lighthouse has been not only a guide but something to behold. The lighthouse, located near Long Point, is among the biggest and brightest on the west coast.

At Point Vicente, from December to May, those of sharp eye look
for gray whales as they migrate south to the warmer waters of
Mexico and then back to their frigid homes in the north.

A spring sunrise.

Sailing off the Peninsula.

The City of Rolling Hills

Rolling Hills is a commerce-free, gated community of 1,900 acres with exquisite, sprawling, California style, one story, ranch type homes. Each is painted white and adorned with a welcoming name sign. Many homes are bordered with equally white board fencing. Tennis courts, swimming pools, and elaborate stables testify to the comfort, pleasure and activities of some two thousand residents listed as among the wealthiest in the nation.

As one slowly drives along the carefully maintained streets, ever mindful of protected horse crossings, it is easy to envy the tree-studded vistas, large open land, and a serene tempo to life.

Open land of Rolling Hills.

Miles and miles of horse trails.

Amid a galaxy of wild flowers.

A tree-studded tranquil vista.

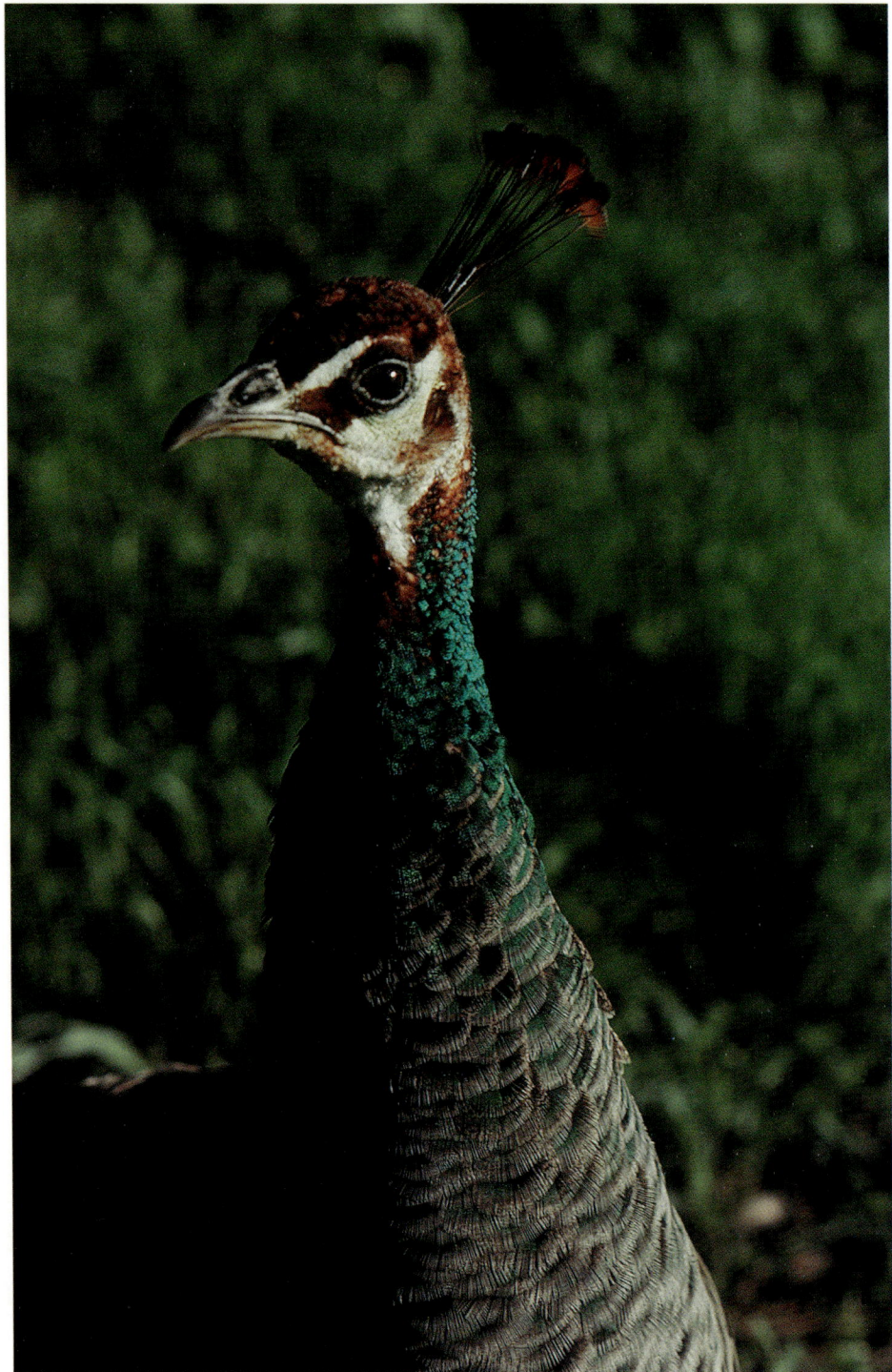

If there were a "Peninsula Bird," it would be the Peacock. Imported to Rolling Hills many years ago, the Peacock originally was settled in an area that become known as Peacock Flats. Today this large pheasant-like bird can be found in all cities of the Peninsula.

Admired by many for its crested head, long brilliant blue and green tail feathers, marked with eye-like iridescent spots, which can be spread proudly in a fan type form, the peacock is equally loathed by numerous others for its general nuisance and noisy screams.

The Rolling Hills Country Store and Post Office—where a bit of history remains.

Palos Verdes Estates

On the western side of the Peninsula, reaching down to the shore of the Pacific Ocean, lies Palos Verdes Estates, the first of the cities to be incorporated and still possessing a strong commitment to protect its cherished rural character. On entering Palos Verdes Estates from the north, a dramatic change is experienced. Congested traffic of nearby freeways and large cities is left behind. An extremely beautiful pastoral setting is maintained in its natural state to preserve an atmosphere that sharply contrasts with the hustle and bustle of Los Angeles just minutes away.

Here 14,000 residents generally have eschewed horses, opting for almost 1,000 acres of permanent parkland. Their magnificent custom homes of Mediterranean style architecture, with red tiled roofs, are reminiscent of the French Riviera. Many offer sweeping views of the ocean as its waves beat on the shore all the way north to Malibu.

The striking marble La Fontana Del Neptuno has become a Peninsula landmark. Located in the square at Malaga Cove Plaza since 1930, this replica of its famed bronze ancestor in Bologna, Italy, aptly represents the figure of Neptune as he holds his three pronged spear, symbolic of his power over mermaids, dolphins, cupids, sea horses and genies.

The Neighborhood Church is one of the most impressive and picturesque of all churches on the Peninsula. The Church occupies what was once a stately Italian Villa situated on the ocean at Malaga Cove. The grounds, flower gardens and walkways, open to the public, are still meticulously maintained.

Sunset in Palos Verdes Estates

For the young of heart, the splendor of vistas that nature
provides at sunset is nothing short of dramatic.

A Sunday ride on the Palos Verdes North trail.

High on a hill overlooking the dramatic sweep of the bay stands the La Venta Inn, known world-wide for its gorgeous architecture. Few Peninsulans have not filled its rooms with laughter and life at social events and romanced in its gardens. Planned in the tradition of a Spanish seaside hostelry, its Mediterranean design and arresting tower meld into a very natural setting. This unusual, lovely place speaks loudly for the special nature of the entire Palos Verdes Peninsula.

La Fuente de Los Ninos, or The Children's
Fountain, graces the Lunada Bay Plaza.

Lunada Bay, perhaps the finest bay on the Peninsula.

Lunada Bay tidepools at sunset.

Craggy shores looking north from Golden Cove.

Flat Rock Point with Bluff Cove.

A rare look at snow capped mountains in the background.

Flat Rock Point, with its steep and rugged cliffs, offers a
contrasting glimpse of nearby bustling Los Angeles.

City lights in the distance bring reality to the tranquility
of life on the Palos Verdes Peninsula.

At Rocky Point, one is reminded by the rusting hull of the Greek freighter, Dominator, that below the beauty of the sea and its enticing coves still lie dangerous reefs that demand the respect of those commanding passing ships.

The imposing St. Francis Episcopal Church, situated
in a quiet, remote setting in Palos Verdes Estates, is
one of the oldest churches on the Peninsula.

Beautiful pepper trees and the famed eucalyptus trees
grace the meticulously maintained Palos Verdes
Country Club golf course.

Malaga Cove offers Peninsula beach goers easy access to miles
of sandy beaches from adjoining Redondo Beach northward.

Rolling Hills Estates

Rolling Hills Estates gives away its equestrian lifestyle by keeping hitching posts in front of the city hall for the convenience of visitors. This close knit community of 8,000 residents covers four square miles. It takes pride in twenty-five miles of horse trails, off-road jogging and bike paths, and a view of the Los Angeles skyline without equal.

The city maintains six parks, a tennis club and riding stables. Facilities at Ernie Howlett Park, the largest of the parks, include professionally designed tennis and handball courts, a 3.4 mile running track, a bicycle path, a regulation handball court, and multiple purpose athletic fields.

Since its inception, the residents have been united in their commitment to maintain a rural residential atmosphere characterized by the rolling hills of the Peninsula, vast open spaces, and white rail fences.

An equestrian community.

More than 100 trails on the Peninsula wander in and
out of the canyons and hills, protected from the wind
in the winter and the heat of the summer. Riders on
paths along city streets in Rolling Hills Estates present
constant reminders of this rural life.

A ride through Chandler Park.

The South Coast Botanical Gardens

One of the world's first environmental gardens developed over a landfill, the colorful South Coast Botanical Gardens offer the visitor two hundred species of birds and numerous varieties of plants, flowers and trees.

At public and private riding arenas, the very best of the nation's horses and riders are challenged to display their beauty and athletic skills. The nationally celebrated Portuguese Bend Horse Show, held at Ernie Howlett Park, features champions competing for blue ribbons as funds are raised for local charities.

Bougainvillea in full bloom.

San Pedro and WorldPortLA

Early settlers knew the "Peninsula" as including the port town of San Pedro. Today San Pedro and its harbor remain part of Los Angeles, which many years ago ordained itself the man-made WorldPortLA, a premier U.S. gateway for commerce. Nevertheless, the intrinsic beauty and activity of the harbor and San Pedro, at the Peninsula's eastern borders, contribute to the "special nature" of the Palos Verdes Peninsula. Residents look down on the intense ocean commerce, the historic charm, and, in the evening, the many sparkling lights.

Angel's Gate Lighthouse, at dawn, guides ships through the breakwater into the Los Angeles Harbor.

Fishing boats, at dockside, ready their nets for
traditional sea journeys.

Point Fermin Lighthouse

The proud Point Fermin pioneer lighthouse evokes memories of other days, long passed. The lighthouse and surrounding grounds reward the imaginative visitor with images of ships being guided through treacherous waters by its winking lights. First oil lamps, then strong electric candle power, reached out for miles to ships carefully treading their way to the safety of the large harbor. Dark since World War II, colorful and dramatic stories are buried in the lighthouse's long history.

The Point Fermin Lighthouse as seen by passing ships.

Royal Palms Beach

The scenic beauty of the recently renovated Royal Palms Beach now brightens the harbor area of the Peninsula. It is located at the foot of White's Point, where only memories remain of the White's Point Hot Springs and Health Resort, whose sulfur water enticed visitors from all over the world. A forty-room hotel of Spanish style, complete with an 18-hole golf course, offered an idyllic recreational setting from 1923 until 1933 when failure of the financial markets and the Long Beach earthquake combined to crumble it.

Day's end.

About the Authors

Mary Donovan has been a serious photographer for many years. She has worked in almost all fields of photography, but most of her recent attention has been devoted to the natural beauty of the seascapes and landscapes of the Palos Verdes Peninsula that change daily from sunrise to sunset. Her photos have been complimented and recognized commercially, and Peninsula residents have admired them in publications and at numerous public exhibitions.

Ted Bruinsma, an attorney and businessman, has been active in all aspects of Peninsula life since 1960. In retirement he has devoted much of his time to writing novels and poetry about America's culture and government. His most recent book, *Foresight Capacity* (1996), received special recognition from the National Association of Futurists.